SCHIRMER'S LIBRARY
OF MUSICAL CLASSICS

Vol. 2150

T0087316

BEETHOVEN
SELECTED PIANO PIECES

FOR UPPER INTERMEDIATE LEVEL

14 Selections from
Bagatelles, Sonatas, Variations and more

ISBN 978-1-5400-8985-4

G. SCHIRMER, *Inc.*

DISTRIBUTED BY

7777 W. BLUEMOUND RD. P.O. BOX 13819 MILWAUKEE, WI 53213

Visit Hal Leonard Online at
www.halleonard.com

Contact us:
Hal Leonard
7777 West Bluemound Road
Milwaukee, WI 53213
Email: info@halleonard.com

In Europe, contact:
Hal Leonard Europe Limited
42 Wigmore Street
Marylebone, London, W1U 2RN
Email: info@halleonardeurope.com

In Australia, contact:
Hal Leonard Australia Pty. Ltd.
4 Lentara Court
Cheltenham, Victoria, 3192 Australia
Email: info@halleonard.com.au

CONTENTS

26   Allegretto in C minor, WoO 53

6   Bagatelle in C Major, Op. 33, No. 2

11   Bagatelle in G Major, Op. 119, No. 6

14   Bagatelle in G Major, Op. 126, No. 1

16   Bagatelle in G minor, Op. 126, No. 2

20   Bagatelle in E-flat Major, Op. 126, No. 3

22   Bagatelle in C minor, WoO 52

3   Bagatelle in A minor "Fur Elise," WoO 59

30   Rondo in A Major, WoO 49

35   Sonata No. 8 in C minor, Op. 13 "Pathétique"

51   Sonatina in E-flat Major, WoO 47, No. 1

60   Sonatina in C Major, WoO 51

73   7 Variations on "God Save the King," WoO 78

66   5 Variations on "Rule Britannia," WoO 79

BAGATELLE
in A minor
"Für Elise"

Ludwig van Beethoven
WoO 59

Poco moto

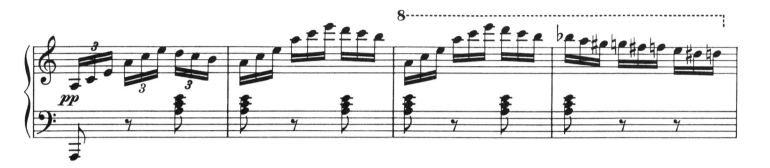

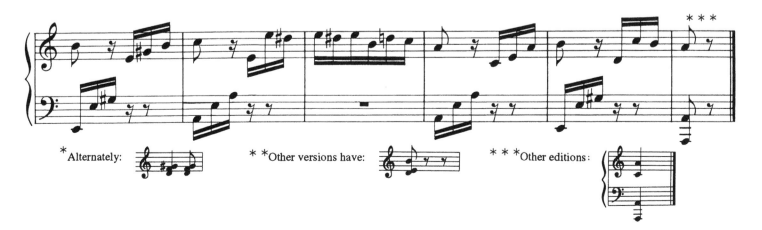

*Alternately: * *Other versions have: * * *Other editions:

BAGATELLE
in C Major

Ludwig van Beethoven
Op. 33, No. 2

Scherzo
Allegro (♩=63.)

Minore (Trio I)

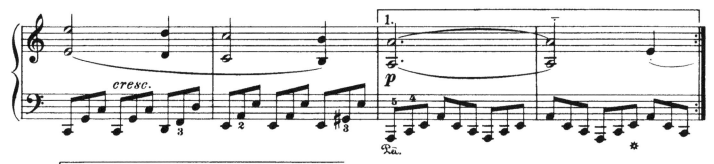

(Trio II)

Coda.

BAGATELLE
in G Major

Ludwig van Beethoven
Op. 119, No. 6

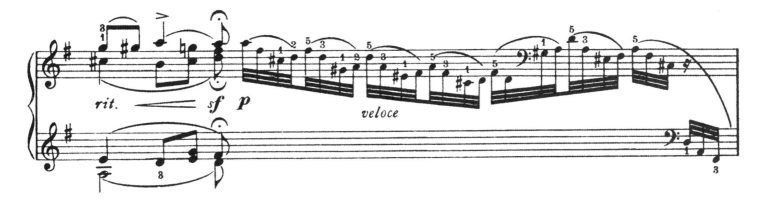

molto leggieramente

a tempo

cresc.   un poco ritard.   *p*

stringendo il tempo

13

L'istesso tempo

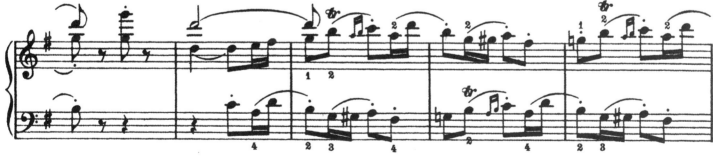

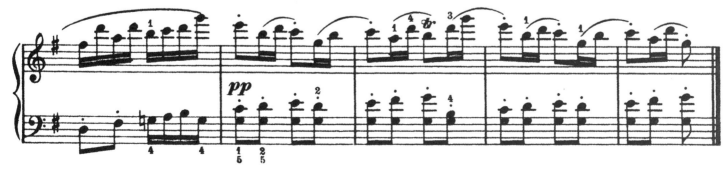

BAGATELLE
in G Major

Ludwig van Beethoven
Op. 126, No. 1

Andante con moto
Cantabile e compiacevole

L'istesso tempo

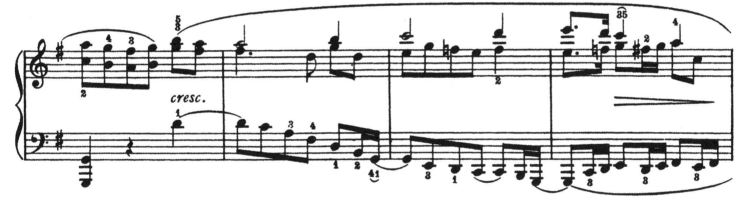

La seconda parte due volte

BAGATELLE
in G minor

Ludwig van Beethoven
Op. 126, No. 2

Allegro

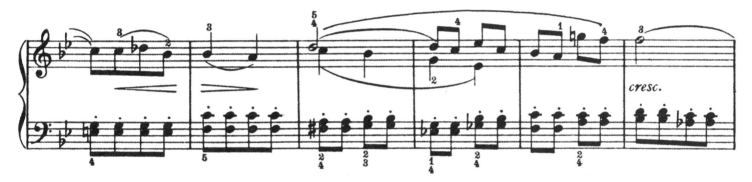

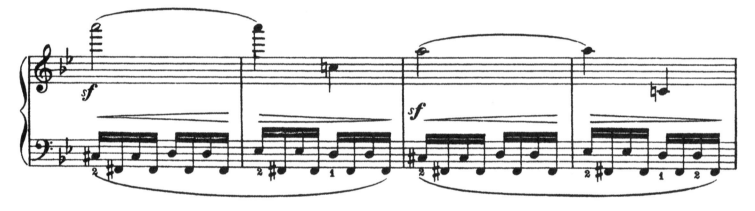

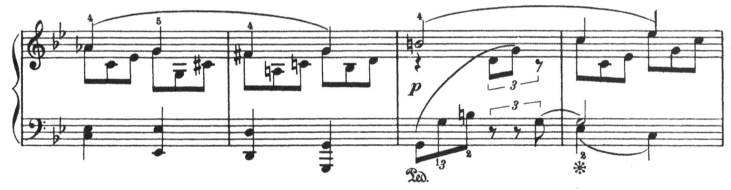

BAGATELLE
in E-flat Major

Ludwig van Beethoven
Op. 126, No. 3

Andante (♪ = 104)
Cantabile e grazioso

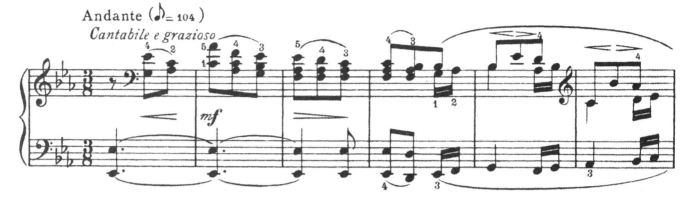

BAGATELLE
in C minor

Ludwig van Beethoven
WoO 52, No. 1

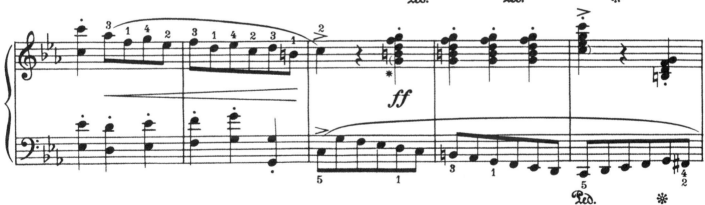

*For players whose hands are too small to negotiate these chords, the editor recommends the omission of the low notes.

24

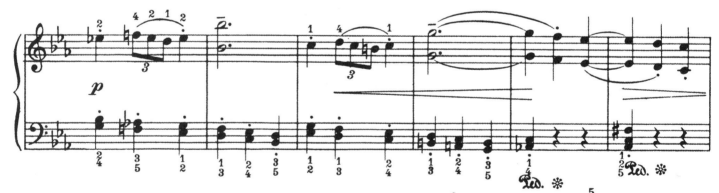

Trio

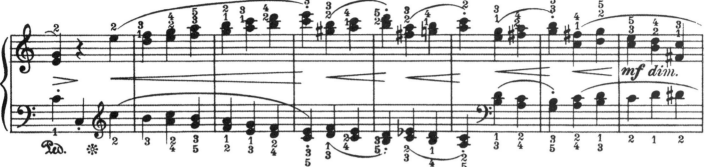

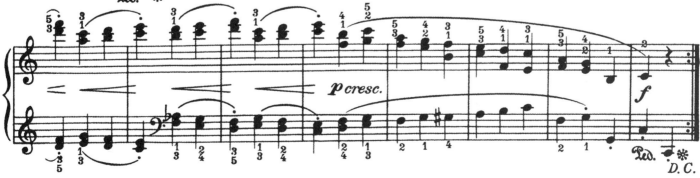

D.C.

ALLEGRETTO
in C minor

Ludwig van Beethoven
WoO 53

Maggiore

sempre legato

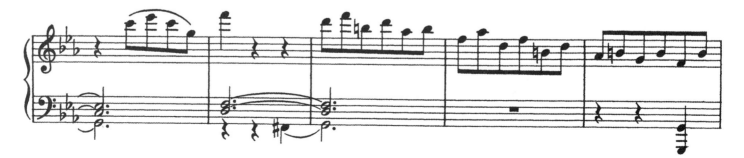

*Compare this measure with m.39.

RONDO
in A Major

Ludwig van Beethoven
WoO 49

Allegretto

*Editor suggests:

Dedicated to Prince Carl von Lichnowsky

SONATA
in C minor
"Pathétique"

Edited by Carl Krebs

Ludwig van Beethoven
Op. 13

attacca subito il Allegro.

Allegro di molto e con brio.

38

Tempo I.

attacca subito Allegro molto e con brio.

Allegro molto e con brio.

Adagio cantabile.

cresc.

RONDO
Allegro.

Dedicated to the Princely Archbishop of Cologne, Maximilian Friedrich

SONATINA
in E-flat Major

Ludwig van Beethoven
WoO 47, No. 1

Allegro cantabile

52

Andante

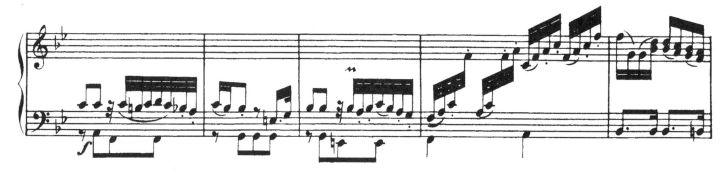

Rondo vivace

SONATINA
in C Major

Ludwig van Beethoven
WoO 51

Adagio

* Completed from this point on by F. Ries.

FIVE VARIATIONS
on "Rule Britannia"

Ludwig van Beethoven
WoO 79

Var. III.

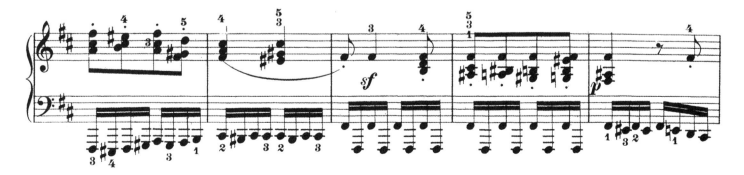

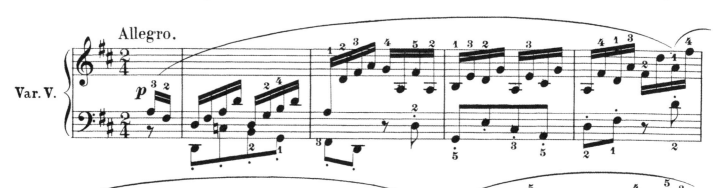

Coda.

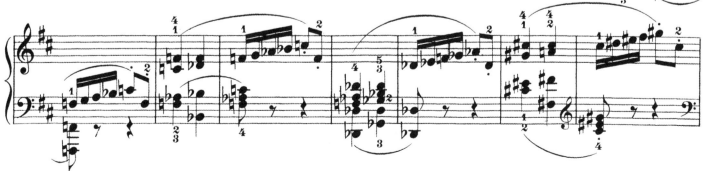

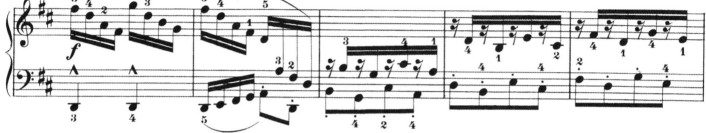

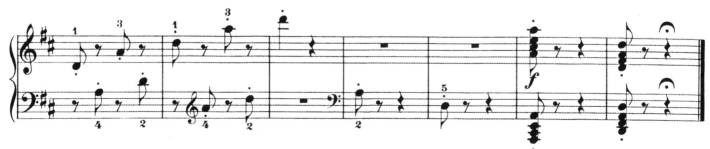

SEVEN VARIATIONS
on "God Save the King"

Ludwig van Beethoven
WoO 78

Tema.

Var.I.

Var. II.

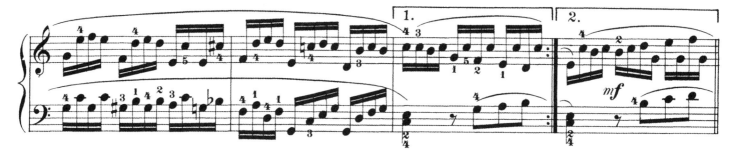

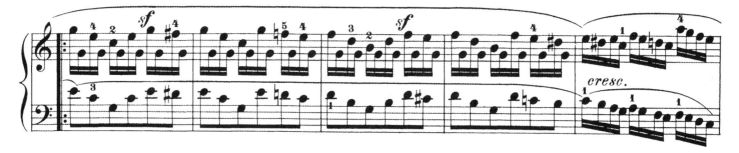

Var. III.

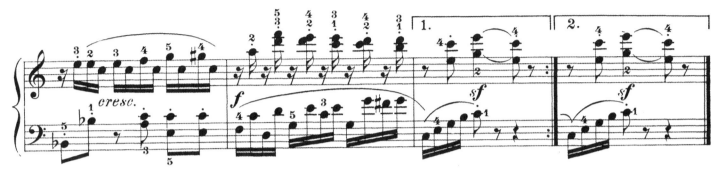

Con espressione.

Var. V.

Allegro:Alla marcia.

Var. VI.

Var. VII.

Coda.

Adagio.

Allegro.